WEST OF THE AMERICAN DREAM

By the same author

East by Southwest

WEST OF THE AMERICAN DREAM

visions of an alien
landscape

poems to read aloud

by NEIL CLAREMON

WILLIAM MORROW & COMPANY, INC.
New York, 1973

for Rose and Golde
in trust of the tree of life

CONTENTS

WEST OF THE AMERICAN DREAM

I

"When you enter thru the crack to the other side of the veil," said the rabbit, "there will be a wind that blows the sun around faster in the sky. You see things by their shadows for when you see the thing itself it is too late and there is no place to hide. Every way you tilt your head there is the surface of the ground and in the distance the sky. It is a place of crystals inside of crystals. And as you travel you will be aware of things on either side both at the same time."

PIPELINE

All the way from El Paso
to Reno—scrambling roads of the desert
I dreamed of a lit match

saw flames shooting
all the way from El Paso to Reno; the long
high pressure gasline

shut down during the coldspell
of '71, I light a cigar sitting on a pump
trespassing

see two young hawks
cut thru each other's circles, more stabbings
in bars of El Paso—

it was a rainy night
in Juarez, the streets deserted, Charlie on
his back with *turista*

something goes stuttering
like a stuck key thru the pipeline: all those
barrio kids at El Paso High

turned on to Lorca,
the knife and the blood, the ballad the John Birch
principal couldn't understand

read by a beautiful girl
her hips swaying, reading the "Cassida
of the Reclining Woman"

staccato in my mind
and she told me her brothers would try
to rape her as she slept:

"Verte desnuda es recordar la tierra,"
"to see you naked is to remember the earth"

good scrambling, the wind
and the hawks, the wind and the match
all that heat.

in broad daylight the form you make
    called into being on the whirl-
        wind, our own eyes deceive us

ages of sand uprooted

    you raise the dead
        with the force of the handtrembler
        an epilepsy of dust

        playful cloven fellow
          your top spinning
        across the fields

(I'm told these are smoke signals
    of the Kachinas of the Peaks
        in which might be a message
of death)

    a matter of chance
        the cone is temporal
          grains of sand

they slip thru our vision, our mind's
   eye as a mirage
      to enter into, held
in our heart's grasp

   when you die you plant
    teeth and bones
       manure and seed.

One who had five bullets from a .38
pumped in him point-blank and went drinking
a week later
had a right to think he was immortal
had a true access. We drew a circle,
who else could I do this with?
in a circle of large cholla to be sure
no one else could enter,
raised the huge sword and drew the pentagram
shadowed in flames,
leapt to and fro Coors-crazed
shouting, "I take in hand the Sword of Power
for defense against evil and aggression"
and the syllables: Zeba-oth, Jah, El, Ekpher-o
then waited nearly shivering;
but what did we expect?
the Esidim, teachers of Christ in the desert
so you could walk thru a crowd of bullets?
yet what appeared surpassed this:
your wife's children
tumbling in the fiery mirror.

PENETRATION

i.

    This is the path
O traveler, on the road from Malkuth to Kether
on the left are

    the thick, stone walls
of Yuma Territorial Prison: bare cells
rusted chains

    rocks being broken with
the whistle of sledgehammers in disembodied hands;
on the right

    the Colorado pours into
the Gulf of California—Alarcón's 3 ships
waiting their rendezvous—head waters
boiling at the gateway

    in the center for students
I talk with a clean-cut Mormon kid about mescaline
and peyote, his father's an agent controlling
the border

    he wants to know
what the world is like in Tucson: my mind
diverted, my eyes following

a dark Mexican girl
carved of obsidian beneath her white dress
of perfect proportion.

ii.

   We go down to the water
she raises a hand and covers the sun's glare
water calming, wind in her voice

   she wants to marry
a spiritual man—abjures me, a man on business
not of the knife

   her pristine lips reveal
a mystery I cannot hold; what is there she wants—
what bird or snake to rend virgin fruit?

   falling south, churning masses
of black scorpions in cells of Hermosillo jails,
their lobo men

   and women with vaginal fangs;
the river moving, swirling 'round a sail of rock
she smiles, and her teeth flash white.

electricity is the catalyst
    and it's out
        in the calm
I am left at home with myself

birds silent
    branches still
        a frightened katydid
my balls rattle in their scrotum
    the fuck wells up inside
        a time of 2 Emilys I've known

from their graves the rage, bowing of plants
    wind's howling thru liquid glass
        heat lightning and heft of thunder
that never comes
    conflagration of rain
        wall after wall
the yellow glow that seems to come from the ground
    colder and colder

        lightning flares
            startling another eye
              with violet . . .

if it's quick enough it enters the long crack
    gathering at the edges
        then crashing like a wave
leaving behind thousands of singing frogs . . .

    on the other side I will make a circle
        storm cannot enter
           for a dry soul is best
but when streams seep thru
        will pan them for gold.

At dark or in the harsh light
paths will lead to a dead end;
the four well-dressed women alone in a bar
I'd turned into by the railroad tracks,
cold as the steep box canyon
when it's too late to turn back;
no where to climb but a bar stool
a woman refusing my night-cap of tequila
four women laughing, fondling each other,
a man could die of thirst here;
washroom pictures of women drinking
reversed upon themselves, a chill
sacrilegious feeling: bats screeching
things a child fears in the darkness
all the exits bolted with long
red fingernails; but I can assume
a more awesome shape, Centaur,
the ability to move thru the walls.

One son dead of suicide & a daughter
missing in the white world
old woman watches us walk
at the homesite with her true son
for we are still the enemy.

Soon her youngest daughter
comes over a rise herding their horses
bareback; the old woman is pleased
and holds the other one's
baby to her heart, smiles at it
a fearsome smile
the child must endure.

She leads our gaze to a cloud
her words sound with no sense to us
yet shades of meaning in her voice
open to us—shapes in the amorphous
form of the single cloud:

two lovers wrestle face to face
arms twined, legs kicking at the sky;

one was dark & one was light
and as they wrestle they whirl
the cloud shape to an embryo . . .

our vision of the foetal one, was it
then? I felt my shell break
a glutinous sweat
slipping ice cold from my skin,
as I tried to learn those sounds
her words had made.

II

"There," said the rabbit, "I could see no clouds in the sky and I could see for great distances by tilting my head, yet the sky was darker than blue. Everywhere there were kangaroo-like creatures that were also like rats and they could live without ever drinking water. They scurry around the deserted plains where the plants are shriveled and full of thorns. Homes of man are covered with dust and there are frightening things: they are not coyotes, or snakes, or bobcats and hawks. They are things that are all bones—cat shapes that have wings, man forms with heads of horses or cows, dogs with long serpent bodies —as if all the things that had been dead long in the desert had re-formed themselves with whatever was at hand. The bones without flesh."

SCAVENGERS

    Those who would be hustlers
have assembled in the lungs, their breath lingering
on the spine of a broken neck

    they are so small and common
it's hard to notice them among the many on the voyage
thru the carcass of the giant

    who is a cow: they cry
more acres, there must be more acres, teach us the way
from the heart to the brain—where are developments of
the locusts

    or the crickets who fiddle
for our queen where she is having her coiffure
in the web of a black widow

    who has eaten her third
husband by the kidneys, not a tear of blood shed
as the hourglass turned;

    this incomprehensible world
of flesh decomposing in the dream of a turkey vulture
it rises from the roadside

from the world as a dead cow
and lingers in the sky 'til a jet plane belches
a buzzard in its gut

the food-chain cycle
is not humorless, the young are born they eat
thru the living and the dead

on the strange voyage
thru the carcass of the giant who is a cow
with their language of motors

of spare parts, they
are who we have become—this, the night of wings
around a yellow bulb.

I know that man's heart beats faster
as he thrusts,
the woman coils and recoils in waves;
of cycles and rhythms
naked in the eye of the summer storm
inside for winter rains;
even the *duende* comes and goes!

Having forgotten names of the people
of an ancient civilization,
a stem emerging from my cranium
I must do the exercise of plants
exhale oxygen at night;

the spirit to ferment in the flesh
as in laboratories of old.

D. H. said, "Retreat to the desert
and fight. Fight to protect yourself
but with yourself be strong and at peace."
Those hard interiors . . . cities in rock.

So little changing but the angle
of the sun, the way up
and the way down are one and the same,
one path while we walk
in the still point of a late summer's eve.

Horses of Superstition matted with thorns
tensions of roots, I keep the faith . . .
no way now for the man who kept snakes
the pre-dawn reptile in lava mountains
it's too late to deal in pebbles and stones
for the woman, his wife who let them
crawl up her arm,
an open range with hidden canyons
always behind;
and returning from San Diego, this couple
frustrated at every turn, jobless
taking the children to their own parents
as if for a weekend;
we found them together in the foetid air
black, acid-eaten where fangs struck—
the contorted hari-kari of nerves
overgrazed like the desert
in cold, dark sleep with open eye dreams;
the snakes kept like jewels
sand-tracks returning to their brethren
in the pass, their home.

EARTH MOTHER

She has chosen to leave
her cliff-dwelling, neurotic scuttle of insects
where all the bats she knows are vampires

if it weren't for lice
she'd nurse her sister's babies, crazy with that
winsome smile

she descends from her lair
her sore, swelled nipples brush the burr grass
of the Southwestern plain:

she would have her children
but prefers love entering from behind, having eaten
her own with the afterbirth

revenge & revenge on her lover
director of a film on wolves who married a virgin
and leaves her to rejection on city outskirts

she prefers windy days
damp sands of arroyos, the night of rains—her tears
shed for a promised ring

and the darkness, where
as a wolf or woman she approaches your children
with bared teats and fangs

'copters of the ranchers
like hounds in the distance, the odor of her human
defecation offends

passers on the highway
trying to steer thru her wailing storms, they
cry, they cry out

in nomine patris . . .

Meditation: FOR REDISCOVERING QUARTZ

Mystic? or, a freedom of the mind
to wander

once, over the phone after they
said an operation was a success
last words of her grandmother
were

to take care of her dearest girl

long before we were to be married
how did she know?
this woman from Texas I'd never seen

is it that light shoots out of the eyes
as Donne mentions; can
it become darts of quartz
an image reawakening old myths
from the plains

darts of quartz sent by gods
or enemies—
in the latter case they had to be
sucked out

23

wondering who these gods might have been
who used crystal
I find that it abounds
has a propensity to hold gold

and this has caused minor expeditions
or more often a shaped piece of quartz
left under a pillow.

This is a lonely place
three mountain ranges drift into the sky
held by telephone and power lines,
fields of green alfalfa and cotton
along the roads: Silverbell to the old mine
Pima Farms to the guest ranches
and unpaved trails to Cortaro
an old man with a stray dog
his bent sahuaro-rib cane
bearing a scant weight the wind
bends around;
I haven't seen a face beneath his brown hat
not at any hour—
it's so common to pass him, I wonder
if he ever stops winding out of the washes
among these barbed hills,
but then those owls that swoop up at night
I never found their homes;
I admire his steady gait, the lean shadow,
he's taken to waving, hardly
a nod as I pass &
I've begun to wave back at him.

Theirs is the life
of sitting on telephone poles, of wires they can't
care to understand

only the waves and the hills
that fade into blue, flowing as blood in flesh
and veins in flesh in skeins of blinking lights

colors of the mouse,
the rabbit, the sparrow who live the stable life
and die at home—and die so easily in the fell
swoop at home

"we sleep in the heat
of afternoons when all is bleached like salt
along the marshes; we winter in the desert

always the winter in the same
place in the desert, tho there's a price on our heads
their bounty; but ours

is the bounty of harvests,
hunters' raids on the outskirts—leaving that
which reproduces, taking only what we need, not
always the best"

the towns have locked their doors
have set out their police, fields patrolled while
the looting goes on by unfamiliar faces

"we leave in the spring
when fruit ripens on the trees of the marshes to
have our young in the opening of the year

and will return by the course
of the sun with talons sharper than ever: in winter,
only the fittest survive."

III

"It is flesh that these things are after. If they catch you, you must run thru their teeth before they grind you for they have no stomachs to hold you. There is nothing else to fear, still it is best that you go at night for then it is quiet and you can rest from the things that would prey upon you here on this side."

BORDERS

Reapers holding the scythe
waist high, Karma of the fields, the wheels spin
across West Texas steppes

I close my eyes
and am on the other side of a county line
my wife beside me

the Alamo thru the trees
strolling the banks of the old mission town, moon
above and there's a cop

coming up the river
Guardia Civil style in an outboard motorboat;
your strange birthplace—once I promised
to take you to Spain

the palms, tho, belong to
Brownsville, Texas, and the brick Presbyterian church
as your brother marries

afterwards in Matamoros
on the far side of the Rio Grande, café aura
so much like Granada for a moment

31

I didn't realize our age,
that time would pass as the bus thru Brownsville
by the wedding of a day past

only giant river cockroaches
there on the bridge over the border, unmindful
of the customs gate

when even the bus driver
thinks he's a South Texas sheriff: at Corpus Christi
then San Antonio again

a charm of paranoia
where you might have married a 2nd lieutenant;
in the mirror where eyes of the driver exude
gestapo's carbon monoxide

whatever country this is!
still in love, rivers flowing on to Pacific shores
curios bought at the Continental Divide.

In these states where the ranchers
beat their children to submission
and courts grant them custody,

it can but tear at the whole fabric
to see small Indian children
guided by smiling nuns!

these foster children
coming to the watershed of fear
have traded the animal messengers
and the skin-walker for Hell,

if this were the time for adoption . . .

first, the children must be returned
to their parents
for they are adorable

the rivers must be returned to their tribes
teachers must go to the villages
on the grazing land;

we must plan this turning back
a revolution.

33

Tho days have passed in grey clouds
    you will dance for us
        dust of the veil
cleansed from the air

you pirouette in the wind and green vapors
    rise from rich ground
        where will be a scent

to go by

    for it's tempting to walk in the coolness
        before you
deceptive arroyos lurking.

    My dance won't bring you back
        altho I dance
            the joy unbroken
    which is not of the body.

You must come after the long heat
    flowers open to
        then thrice in a week
or not at all
    as in the past
        when it poured
and you made treaties with fire.

SALT RIVER

In a black inner-tube
swirling on the cold currents after nightfall:
ravens, vultures—blackbirds of red wing
of white wing

    only owls seeing in the darkness
leaders of our nation forming a coalition
of the worst elements

    I see a Victorian mansion
on a barren desert hill, towers and spires
serving as roosting places

    two blacks sitting at a bus stop
this could be anywhere, a power plant, city lights
dimming starlight

    and they are not waiting,
they have been loving in the park here in Tempe
with a song on their lips

    heard from the black birds
at the source, black mud becoming sand where
the Salt River no longer flows

"she raised bared arms in uncontrollable desire
to touch the sky, and at the same time swift shadows
darted out of the earth"

I listen to the salt settle
the water rising into the air amidst the whirr
of monstrous turbines

daughter of the black swan
gliding brazen around the fearful mansion, who
would come to walk with you?

evoking earth shadows,
the river trickling to unnatural ends, is there
a choice between the dam and the flood?

leaders of our nation
forming a coalition of the worst elements, only
owls seeing in the darkness.

TWICE I CONSIDER MY COUNTRY

A raccoon lies quietly in the sun,
trickle of a river
between furrows of sand,
this is life
it has need of water
how rare to see one in the desert;
by glowing charcoal, bottles
shot up in the mouth of an Indian cave,
the red opal of blood
at the temple of a raccoon . . .
the Santa Cruz
bends from the highway
an odor of processed sewage
in the breeze,
I am looking for boundaries
it's like crawling again.

Obscured by sunflowers
wild olive branches, their paint gone
only ribs in the sand, 1940 models
the war babies
shore up the road;
I hear their dashboard radios blaring again
this same old war
they shake

as the cars keep coming;
they have not abandoned America
like the river
slowly they go underground.

gourds at vine's end in the cracked dry mud
    of a winter's rain
        try the exercise
of going and coming
    thru the hollow in the stomach

bend with the scythe, or age
    mowing of the bees
      at flowers is not
the cat's mowing at nests
    of curve-billed thrashers.

      in the black hoods of 3 buzzards
        in the thickest cove in the hills
          sight thy grave.

snakes after eggs, their side-winding
    thru reeds where the well leaks
      is where you find
death's rattle.
    Out of the rottings of summer cabbage
      come butterflies and white fall corn.

sad
    or happy
        searching both sides of the mountain
be at once wet and dry
    for there is a crack in-between
        for coming and going.

DAWN ENTRY

At sunrise
there is an escalator of light
to ride out on the waves,
and among beer cans
an apple crate, smell of rotting fish
our anniversary;

reaching to fulfill herself, she is
becalmed and will sleep late
as I kick driftwood
with all the tenderness left in the world:

behind me, a dark continent westward
its silver dagger
poised,
the gleam of it!

nights, hearing the wild boars run blind
I've felt no fear, and
wanting to be back in the Sonoran desert
I recall it was she
who collected fragments of seashell
fossils of anemones
in the coolness of dawn;

she could be the sun reaching
over the ocean,
her sleep is that ancient
murky and deep, oh
as the tide comes in.

IV

"I saw in the night under the stars— as only at dark is it bright—the great rehearsals of the strongest spirits. In small groups they would meditate on the things they would become when they crossed back thru the veil. This was the world of flesh to be, and in watching once for a long time I could see flesh forming on the lights that were spirits, and their places would have dark spots on them. I could begin to see shapes that could be recognized on this side and sometimes would shudder at the sight. At times over there, you can hear the transfer of energies which is like the sound of water passing thru roots."

THE MESAS

i.

    Along the Via Americana
as if horsepower at my command were enough
to enter the city, the multitudes poured
from 400 Gallup bars

    but the relay stations
were all burned, the arrows long charred,
bodies of horses bloated—with hooves
frozen in the air

    in mud and snow, Indians
stagger across the field, in the end-zone
the fullback throws the feathered bonnet
to the ground

    thunder across red mesas
I await the final score, the fans cheering
the ways of the cavalry;

    'don't call the thunder's name
lightning can follow you!'

ii.

Quit work, their pick-up
overturned in the trees, moaning softly
too drunk to get up

4 Zuñi are freezing to death;
in the morning Pat and I return to the spot
find some blood frozen in snow

view of scrub oak, juniper
and piñon, sheep dogs and a stockade: apparitions
in the raw silence;

Jim Beam in his eye
Harry Bahe looks at the white girl who could pass,
    "you listen 'cause I know," he says
and I want to be friendly
    "drink to get dead drunk or not at all."

'If you weave during lightning
it makes the patterns in the sky.'

iii.

From the eye of
the old sand painter grains of colored sand
design an icon

"Leave it be," I say
as finishing he tramples the painted earth
"You crazy?" he says

    we get together at Eddie's bar
Pat, Harry Bahe, the painter, each immersed in
the delicious white girl who could pass for Indian

    leaving, I picked up
a Navaho and his daughter; they laugh all the way
up the open road—tell me to stop in a place
where there's nothing

    and get off walking . . .

AT CANYON DE CHELLY

If only I had a prayer rattle
to take home
from where water runs over
smooth stucco rock, and mornings
the sun glows
across the high mesa country
of this forbidden city;

we hear voices of children we cannot see
and iron wheels;
it seems the tribes just move thru
farm the land awhile,
the Cliff Dwellers have moved out
for good;

their homes remain
on snaking chasms of river-honed
office buildings, windows cut
above the autumn trees
and tall grass. You may miss seeing
messages carved in rock:

but too many eyes have peered in
intimidating, I fear,
presences who keep the world's plan,
and at dawn their rope ladders
are not let down. Listen
to the children playing & the wagon wheels;
notice, to the east
the horses have no riders.

That alien woman, blue eyes, black hair
taunting me in the past,
I thought I saw her tonight:
she wore a Mexican wedding dress
and threw small rocks against the stone chapel
in the desert;
my mind's going—stellar fragments drift
between familiar constellations—
I think I will live forever
and see her in the future, south of here
on the Papago sanctuary;
in anger you see the moon has a sad face
an orange glow
in love's quiet nocturne
it's evident tomorrow will be hot
something in the sadness of this face—
dark craters of its complexion rising
above the cloistered mountains—
which we know of night, her goddess
Hecate who reigns, you and I!

Meditation: FOR A MAYAN DOG

coming upon an ancient piece
surreptitiously
one delights in the realm of intrigue

beginning with the object of money
     or if it were stolen
from what source?
perhaps smuggled directly out of
ashes and mud

with broken ears, and eye-sockets
where jewels were inset;

I would figure astrologers
who could draw
perfect calendars of the nine planets
would render a dog less like
a pig

or is it a matter of words?
the secret less revealed in what is
said

than in the arrangement
thru which 'in the assembly
when the final etching is unknown
given vague intuitions
the form takes shape'

revealing a new element
unknown in nature

. . . and I don't know what it is for
giving rise to the problem
of where to keep it,

tho, I was given instructions to behold it
for a constant time
until what it was used for in the past
left no alternatives

I ask if it were knocked off
its place on the window-sill
would it be broken?

Hat mountain's smashed under the pick-ax
quartz veins bleed in the sun,
the grave robbers have found their pyramid;
I take their rusted hammer in hand
hold it against the shadow of a 50 ft. cactus
blot out the crimson vulva at the top;
always the new-born eye blinks
and cannot see
one seed in a thousand will germinate;
the wooden ribs wrench, weak
of their weight, one slat cracking
after another—my bones flinch
at the tendons, my vertebrae weld to the spine
of the stationary life;
the plant falling to its own shadow
with the memory of two centuries of survival.

We can leave this house to termites
my body doesn't live here
or separate from yours;
I hear them munching in the dry adobe straw,
what valence in weathered rail beams?
I can't reconcile the summer cloud
of blank heat that leaves me
tilted back endlessly in a reclining chair
with that angle of streaked clouds
beneath the first, cold North Star;
each angle an energy, constant buzzing
and the trees cry out;
here in my retreat, a winter twilight
dark foil of the day and hour inside me;
my mind is the house: cold tile floors
a knotty pine ceiling, weighed upon
by the ghosts of Fat Fuzzel and Mugs, hair
all over the walls, scampering on the roof
stucco cracks . . .
Please don't clean our love away; OCCUPADO,
you've known me
I'm the man who travels a lot.

OUT-RIDERS

In the last refuge of
mountain islands, it's told the frost is less
bitter than despair

where bighorns have gone
they live with the silence, beggar of hope, and stars
too clear for other eyes

the rabbits, or men who cannot
own their clothes as they change at each season
with the stain of the cover

the foremost of them
had to be shot for his people starved and raged
with whiteman's sickness; he held

the world could be compared
to the turning of a wheel whose center was every-
where—or lost in the Chiricahuas

El Tigre in a cave when sons
whose fathers give them shotguns blast shadows
too quick for their vision

for the Maccabees were coyotes
hunted by the legions of Rome which have spread,
as the Egyptians predicted, to the western lands
of the dead

even the rabbit running the gamut
of his circle is the out-rider is a coyote around
the edge of the rim

cautious to the windscent
eyes dim, ears overgrown, he trusts to the sixth sense
the total of the others

& what you hear is not the coyote
but the rabbit who has taken over the voice
to be heard in that body;

on the distance
the voices in the canyons, in ancient rocks and
water flowing at the center.

V

"Flesh," said the rabbit, "belongs to the class of substance like the pulp in cactus. It is the veil that is the membrane that takes blood from the dying as they leave and gives it to the living as they return. You must only go thru the cracks in the veil or you will forfeit your blood. It is hard to find the strength to enter a crack. A tremor or a storm may help for on this side all is diluted with light."

CAHUILLA NIGHTS

On the lonely drive
from Yuma to L.A. the road ahead narrows around
Banning, one may stop for coffee

offer a sullen Indian a cigar
learn his name is Capt. Ambrosia and wind up driving
him home as he works a cat's cradle

breathing jimsonweed
crunching charcoal sparks fly thru his nose into
the dark cabin of forgetfulness

he speaks of the Mother Lode
at the center where our veins run with a magnetism
to map out our lives

most of his world up and about
at midnight, each animal sound has its precise locale
the mountains take on a clear definition

a bobcat learning its territory
would need to know these things, or a man to find
his way without lights to I-10

the eyes strain, hills
begin to move, the sounds juggle in endless play
the tank near empty

a slap at the face might
dispel uncanny notions in vast desert places
many stars to navigate by

nerves will move with the lay
of the land, and exhausted one might lie down to
pioneer forces of law and order

the catcher-of-spirits
heading on to Eternity like a child coming home
to roost west of the American Dream.

Meditation: FOR RITUAL MUSIC

a dance, freestyle
the temple radiant with flowers
   tho the old mystery is gone
it is still a gathering place

we would redecorate as when
my wedding took place
under an old oak tree   six years
between my sister and me

6, the perfect number of woman's love
the waltz in which
Sagittarius holds Cancer out-
stretched then together around the ring

it is caught up by the old woman
balding but quick and alert
   all laughter and smiles of youth
Babushka, twice married
it seems again she goes thru

the joys of the ceremony

as we play that music
without sentimental strains
so it lives
            in our style

for
    'she wore the same dress
on a day, once again
not so long ago, which thrilled me
as the light came thru the window
in that same way.'

I can't move I stand upwind and still,
the coyote drinks at a leaking pipe
shrill laughter of a pack
echoing off last night;
I know that space turns on itself,
a wild dog
30 ft. from our porch is an entrance
to a cryptic animal world, but
my leg's so bruised I haul it with me
hot day after day!
When she turns she holds me fixed
in her black and white frame—
at this moment of congruence
we stand in fear of traps and poisons
protecting ourselves with daylight—
now she limps toward me
as if I weren't here, a body
for a moment outside time,
and holds her pace to the chaparral
a gift I had.
I am 28 and a half; lame as the coyote
I know the others would kill her.

You must get out of me, there are
others here
who died in this canyon;
I've no desire to kiss the woman
you dream of:
how easily you duped her, this party
people I've never known
I am not at peace continuing your life
your woman sucking at my tongue
where is this apartment?
the lichen cracking
lava rock for soil, a rabbit
drinking dew, buzzard
waiting his agent
the jaguarundi in the inner cycle
of life and death of the canyon
there are ancient ones
I seek.

An old time homesteader
patrols his ranch in a jeep, truck rustlers taking
twenty head a week

Western, American, Apache
and the old lady with faith at the slot machines
service Reno Nevada

or a vacation at Tahoe
another waylay station along my rounds
to reach home

in the coin melting-pot
theft of one-armed bandits at Harrah's place
25 stories under the stars

a Pima girl
frail, thin girl, heard of the witch *ntsi-a-tachi*
writes poems in the style of Vaughan:

> "I saw Eternity the other night
> Like a great ring of pure and endless Light"

it leads me in an astral body
to the romantic honey-moon, elation in the water
and in the skin rag shop

tan, golden, Reno girl
coupling with a ram, Aries beckoning open up
come in

call girls' bruised breasts
for easy credit; faro, roulette, black jack, plush
velvet come-on

the resident Yoga instructor
provides a lesson: sit, cross your legs, hands on
your heels; it works!

I find her
we drive into the pure white snow, green fir
and pine scent

the road curving,
curving again into the pale-face sun.

There are beautiful things
like what possessed us to climb so high
on an evening's walk
which will linger long after us
undressing on a flat rock
the slope of the mountain silhouetted
in the waning sun;
balancing ourselves your breasts fit
under my chest
the rock fortress on top falls into shadow
and I enter that zone
pass thru your cunt as an opening
hands running the slopes of belly and hips
rise to the vantage point where my voice
is as soft as your inner folds
the view embraces us, reaching out
in all directions as we hover on the top
of a ridge, fall
stumble down the twisting trail in the dark
not meeting anyone.

Meditation: FOR OUR FIRST CHILD

a rainbow outside
the time you wore the woven dress
having come from washing your hair
I'm sure it was then

your hair shone and your face
grew more radiant

will it have my wandering nose
or your Scottish hair and soft skin, or
crags in its face?

it was these looming mountains
that brought us together
a memory of a pool we both waded in
a long time ago

new screams will be added to the night,
witches gathering in covens
of darkness

I'm busy making a bone amulet
for the screams will be so innocent
so prey to this current world

and footsteps I must imagine beforehand
here in the carving
which holds the power to survive a life.